Mary Church Terrell

Leader for Equality

Patricia and Fredrick McKissack

Illustrated by Ned O.

❖ *Great African Americans Series* ❖

Enslow Publishers, Inc.

44 Fadem Road	PO Box 38
Box 699	Aldershot
Springfield, NJ 07081	Hants GU12 6BP
USA	UK

To Ching, Bob, and Mary

Library of Congress Cataloging-in-Publication Data

McKissack, Pat, 1944-
    Mary Church Terrell: leader for equality/ Patricia and Fredrick
McKissack : illustrated by Ned O.
      p. cm. — (Great African Americans series)
    Includes index.
    Summary: Simple text and illustrations decribe the life and
accomplishments of this civil rights activist.
    ISBN 0-89490-305-5
    1. Terrell, Mary Church, 1863–1954—Juvenile literature. 2. Afro-
Americans—Biography—Juvenile literature. 3. Civil rights
workers—United States—Biography—Juvenile literature. 4. Social
reformers—United States—Biography—Juvenile literature. 5. Afro-
Americans—Segregation—Juvenile literature. 6. Afro-Americans—
Civil rights—Juvenile literature. [1. Terrell, Mary Church,
1863–1954. 2. Civil rights workers. 3. Afro-Americans—Biography.]
I. McKissack, Fredrick. II. Ostendorf, Edward, ill. III. Title.
IV. Series: McKissack, Pat, 1944– Great African Americans series.
E185.97.T47M35 1991
323'.092—dc20   91-3083
[B]   CIP
                                  AC

Printed in the United States of America

10 9 8 7 6 5 4 3

Photo Credits: Moorland-Spingarn Research Center, Howard University, pp. 4, 8,
14, 18, 20, 24, 27.

Illustration Credits: Ned O., pp. 6, 7, 10, 11, 12, 16, 17, 22, 26, 28.
Cover Illustration: Ned O.

Contents

Mary Church Terrell
Born: September 23, 1863, Memphis, Tennessee.
Died: July 24, 1954, Annapolis, Maryland.

1

The Best of Everything

It was 1863. Mary Eliza Church was born in Memphis, Tennessee. Her parents were Robert and Louisa Church.

Robert Church had been born a **slave**.* Mary was born free! Robert wanted his wife and daughter to have the best of everything.

Robert bought and sold land. Soon he

---

* Words in **bold type** are explained in *Words to Know* on page 30.

was a very rich man. Mary grew up in a grand, old house with big rooms. Her special place was in the flower garden. She enjoyed learning the flowers' names.

In the 1870s unfair laws were being passed. Black people were losing their rights. And the laws didn't help them.

Louisa and Robert separated. Louisa started her own business. Both of Mary's

parents had money. And they loved Mary. But it was not enough to keep the unfair laws from hurting her.

What could they do? At last Robert and Louisa decided to send Mary to Ohio. They would miss her. But in the North she could go to a good school. She would be safe.

Mary Church was very interested in women's rights.

2

Wild Ideas!

The years passed quickly. Mary grew into a beautiful young woman. She was also smart. She was well-liked by her teachers and friends.

Mary **graduated** at the top of her class in 1880. Many of her friends married after high school. But not Mary Eliza Church. She wanted to go to college.

Some people thought that was a wild idea. At that time, not many women went to college—especially not black women.

Oberlin College in Ohio was different from most schools in the 1880s. Men, women, and African Americans went to school together. Lots of people thought that was a wild idea, too.

Mary enjoyed learning about the past and the present. Oberlin was full of new ideas. *Women should have the right to vote!*

Now that was really a wild idea! Mary didn't think so.

In 1884 Mary finished her studies at Oberlin. Her father sent her to Europe in 1888. Mary decided to live there for a while. She studied music and great writings.

In 1890 Mary came back to the United States. She had so many job choices. Come work at Oberlin! Come teach in Alabama! No, come to New York!

Mary had met a young teacher named Robert Heberton Terrell. He lived in **Washington, D.C.** Come marry me, he asked. And she answered yes.

Mrs. Mary Church Terrell was a very beautiful bride. She also worked for equal rights for African Americans and women. Some people thought that was a wild idea. But not Mrs. Terrell.

Mrs. Terrell was very interested in education. She served on the Washington, D.C. school board from 1895 to 1911.

3

Women of Color

In the 1890s neither black nor white women had many rights. They couldn't vote. They couldn't hold **public office**. They couldn't go to some schools or work on some jobs. And **segregation** stopped the races from working or living together.

Mrs. Terrell wrote a friend in 1894: "There should not be segregation in the nation's capital." What could one woman of color do? Plenty!

In 1895 Mrs. Terrell was asked to serve

on the Washington, D.C. **school board**. She worked to make the schools better.

One law she wanted to pass said that all children—boys and girls—had to go to school until age 14.

The men on the school board laughed at her idea. The law didn't pass. But Mary wouldn't give up. She never stopped working for better schools.

Robert Heberton Terrell graduated from Harvard University in 1884. He was asked to be a judge in Washington, D.C. in 1902. Judge Terrell also started The Robert Terrell Law School in Washington. He was a loving husband. He died in 1927.

Mrs. Terrell met other women of color who were working for equal rights, too. In 1896 all the African-American women's groups joined under one name: **The National Association of Colored Women**. Mary Church Terrell was the first **president**. She served from 1896 to 1901.

President Theodore Roosevelt named Robert Terrell a **judge**. He was the first black man to be chosen as a judge in the country's capital.

In 1904 Mary Terrell spoke at the International Conference of Women in Berlin, Germany. She gave her speech in English, German, and French. Her speech was about freedom and equality.

4

It Isn't Fair!

The National Association for the Advancement of Colored People (NAACP) was started in 1909. Mary joined soon after. Men, women, blacks, and whites worked together for the rights of all Americans.

Mrs. Terrell also helped start groups for young college women. Women still belong to these groups today.

In World War I black soldiers fought in

Mrs. Terrell had light skin. Sometimes she would eat at an all-white restaurant. Then she would tell the owner she was black and ask why other African Americans could not eat there. This was her way of showing how unfair some laws were.

5

"It Took Long Enough!"

Mary Church Terrell spoke all over the world. Once when she was in Europe she gave her speech in three languages. People were surprised.

In 1940 she wrote her own life story, *A Colored Woman in a White World*. "I am no better off than the poorest woman of my race," she said. She spent the rest of her life working for the rights of all people.

By 1953 Judge Terrell had died. Mrs.

Terrell was 89 years old. And Washington, D.C. was still a segregated city.

Mrs. Terrell and a group of other blacks went to segregated restaurants. They quietly took seats. And each time, they were asked to leave.

The NAACP helped Mrs. Terrell's

group. They took the case to the highest court in the United States. But the judge ruled that the restaurants could stay segregated.

Still the case helped make people think more about the problem. Soon some

Even when she was very old, Mrs. Terrell still worked for equal rights. Above (center), she is protesting all-white restaurants in Washington, D.C.

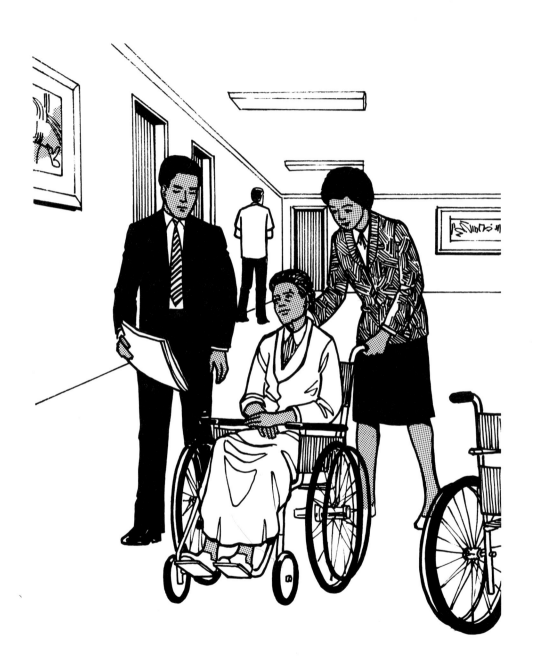

places in Washington chose to end segregation. A law was finally passed ending all segregation in the nation's capital.

Mrs. Terrell was old and very sick. She didn't have long to live. In 1954 the NAACP took another case to the highest court. This time, the judges ruled that schools should not be segregated.

Friends told Mrs. Terrell the good news. She had worked all her life for equal rights. "It took long enough," she said, smiling. Two months later she died in Annapolis, Maryland.

Words To Know

graduate (GRAJ-uh-wait)—To finish all the studies at a school.

judge—The person who decides a court case.

National Association for the Advancement of Colored People (NAACP) —An organization started to help all Americans gain equal rights and protection under the law.

National Association of Colored Women—The name of the organization that included all African-American women's groups.

Oberlin College—A college in Ohio that was not segregated.

president (PREZ-i-dent)—The leader of a country or group.

public office—A position of service to citizens of a city, state, or country.

school board—A group of people who manage the way the schools in the area will be run.

segregation (seg-ruh-GAY-shun)—The separation of people based on race, religion, age, sex, or some other reason.

slave—A person who is owned by another. That person can be bought or sold.

Washington, D.C.—The place where the United States capital is located. D.C. stands for District of Columbia.

Index